Also by Gareth Knight:
Occult Exercises and Practices
The Practice of Ritual Magic

DATE DUE

MY 27 '99	NO 17 05		
DE 6 '99	DE 8 05		
NO 12 99			
DE 8 99			
SE 8 00			
DE 1 '01			
AP 16 01			
MY 10 01			
Nov			
MR 26 02			
MY 21 02			
JE 6 02			
10/3/05			

DEMCO 38-296

12

Magical Images

and the Magical Imagination

A practical handbook for self transformation using
the techniques of creative visualization
and meditation

Gareth Knight

SUN CHALICE
BOOKS
1998

Published 1998 by

SUN CHALICE BOOKS

Copyright © 1998 by Gareth Knight

Publisher's Cataloging-in-publication Data
Knight, Gareth
   Magical images and the magical imagination
    / Gareth Knight
     p.   cm.
   Includes index
   1. Magic
2. Spiritual life   I. Title
BF1611 K 1998   200
ISBN 0-9650839-3-4

Cover and book design by Nicholas Whitehead

Table of Contents

Chapter 1

The Magical Imagination

What is a Magical Image? First we had better ask ourselves what we mean by magic.

As far as we are concerned it is a mental discipline for training certain aspects of our mind so that we can realize our full spiritual potential. So that we can develop a series of natural gifts that perhaps we never knew existed.

There is far more to each one of us than just a physical body. We have instincts and emotions, rational (and irrational) thoughts, and also a sense of moral responsibility. This complex of faculties is sometimes called the soul. And when our soul departs, at the end of physical life, the body decays. It reverts to the basic laws of its physical components when it is no longer a vehicle for soul expression.

Yet there is even more to the soul than what we have just defined. It has other dimensions, inner powers and perceptions that often escape our attention during physical life. We become so consumed with the process of "getting and spending" that these inner powers, perceptions and soul dimensions may never be fully realized. Yet the existence of these higher powers can be proved by experience, given the proper training.

Our souls and bodies are the projection of a yet higher self, whose core is a divine spark of creative spirit. The aim of magical training, then, is to become aware of, and to use, this vast potential that lies within. We may then start to behave like human spiritual beings, rather than as a higher kind of animal.

When we extend the range of our perceptions beyond the world of the physical senses we become aware of an "occult" or hidden world. It is called hidden, or "occult," simply because it is not immediately obvious to our outer senses. Yet it is a perfectly natural world, it has always existed, and is made up of our own higher consciousness as spiritual beings. And also of the higher consciousness of the spiritual beings of others with whom we can communicate.

The way we can extend our awareness of these levels is by a process of "tuning" consciousness. This is very close to the principle of radio. A vast range of radio waves exists all about us, morning, noon and night, and yet we are unaware of it. Although if we have a functioning radio receiver we can tune in to any wavelength of our choice.

Now all of us carry within us a magical radio set. It is a perfectly normal human gift, yet because it is so rarely consciously and properly developed it tends to be classed as "supernatural." This engenders a certain amount of fear and superstition, which are both unnecessary attitudes. Our own inner powers are not of the devil, and nor are those who have developed them bizarrely gifted.

We all have psychic ability. It is our birth right, and it can be trained and developed, just like any other normal skill, be it reading or writing, singing or dancing, playing the violin or swinging from a trapeze. Some people will of course have slightly more or less basic ability than others, but whatever natural talent we have can be cultivated. And we can develop our range of skill to fit our personal needs and aspirations.

We learn to tune consciousness by various forms of meditation, and for the most part this is a training of the imagination. When we do this our imagination ceases to be just an interior picture show of subjective fantasies. It becomes a means of perception. It forms an "inner eye" and "inner ear," and vehicle for other "inner" senses that give us knowledge of the "inner" worlds. And although we may call them "inner," this does not mean that they are only subjective. There is more to the magical universe than mere psychology.

We are accustomed to take the imagination somewhat for granted, even to denigrate it. For many people it seems to be no more than a vehicle for wish fulfillment fantasies, or a subjective refuge for those who seek escape from the "real world." Yet the worlds available through the higher use of the imagination are every bit as real as the physical world.

Indeed we would not be conscious of our existence in the physical world without the power of imagination. And so it will be helpful if we look at the faculty of the imagination a little more closely. It can be usefully divided into three specific functions, under a nomenclature devised by an early pioneer in these matters, the romantic poet and philosopher, Samuel Taylor Coleridge.

The first function of it we may call the *Fancy*, and this is the usual conception of the imagination, as an interior picture show that associates and recombines images that have come to us from the external world. It enables us to manipulate and fashion new ideas in a visual way, whether the medium of expression is a mathematical theorem or a surrealist painting. It is the basis for original and creative thought, how new things get invented, how stories are told, pictures painted, plans made. In other words, it is the stage for the whole process of interior reflection, practically applied.

There is another form of the imagination however, that is equally or even more important, even though we tend to take it for granted or ignore its existence. This is the interpretation into meaningful structures of the raw impressions that come to us, as stimuli to our physical senses, from the physical world.

If a blind man suddenly receives the gift of sight, it is some time before he is able to interpret that sudden blast of light impressions. He has to learn to reconstruct this kaleidoscopic barrage into a series of pictures that make sense. This is an ability that most of us learned in early childhood, to translate sense impressions into a system of representations that we can regard as an ordered world about us.

This unconscious or automatic organizing of sense data is the work of a type of imagination that is so basic and fundamental to our process of physical awareness, that we can appropriately call it the *Primary Imagination.*

There is yet another form of imagination, and one equally difficult to detect unless we know what to look for. It is the type of imagination that interprets the impressions that come to us from the higher worlds.

It tends to work in powerful images and so is particularly appropriate to religious experience and to the arts. These images are generally called symbols, because as well as being images in their own right, they may also stand for something else, something "other" than themselves. They "resonate" with other meanings. They have a certain power or numinous quality about them. This is apparent in the significance we feel about the imagery of certain dreams.

We do not have to be in dream consciousness for this type of imagination to work however. It is to be found wherever a certain fascination is felt about any particular image.

This can be the charisma about a certain person, be they lover or leader, or about a special object, be it religious relic or souvenir of past times. It may be felt in a profoundly moving piece of prose or poetry or drama, or before any great work of art. It can also be associated with places, pilgrim shrines, or sites of scenic grandeur. Something is being represented beyond the surface reality and meaning of the object itself. All this is the province of the *Secondary Imagination*.

The Secondary Imagination works largely through the agency of symbols. There are various grades of symbol, the simplest of which are purely intellectual ciphers, such as mathematical, scientific or other conventional signs that are used as a form of convenient shorthand to represent certain physical quantities, objects or processes. The symbols, however, that we wish to designate magical images, are those that do not merely "represent" something else. A magical image resonates to a higher kind of reality. It carries within itself something that is "not of this world."

By systematic work upon these magical images, in all their rich variety, we may become aware of our own higher selves and the greater world of which they form a part.

Magical images themselves have different powers and purposes, and we can divide them into certain types. One division is between animate and inanimate images, which in turn can be further divided. Animate images may be human or non-human. Inanimate images may be simple objects or complex structures. Please refer to the Table below.

Magical Images and the Magical Imagination

ANIMATE		INANIMATE	

Human	Non-human		Objects	Structures
teachers	animals		numinous artefacts	cosmic maps
ancestors	angels		abstract symbols	landscapes
historical	elementals		pictures	temples
fictional	extra terrestrials			shrines
gods				

Inanimate magical images form a natural sequence rather like a series of Chinese boxes, one within the other. That is to say, we may start by finding our bearings by means of a cosmic chart or map; this leads us to going on a journey through an inner landscape. We may then make our way as pilgrims towards a particular temple or other sacred structure. In this we may find a shrine, wherein may be certain numinous objects.

There is a similar hierarchy of *animate magical images* although in not quite so clear cut a sequence. Small animals, sometimes in the form of "totem animals" may lead us on part of the way. Figures of elemental beings or angels, of various grades, commonly act as guardians or guides to further levels. Any instruction received is likely to come from contacts with human forms, be they spiritual teachers or guides, or personal ancestors, relatives or more widely known historical figures. More exotic contacts can take the form of anything from ancient god forms to visitors from outer space, or may take on the characteristics of well known fictional or legendary characters. Indeed, any form may be encountered which the human imagination is capable of visualizing and using as a means of inspiration or helpful guidance.

Unpleasant images are liable to induce unpleasant experiences but such are likely to occur only in negative circumstances. Such circumstances include debased motives in pursuing this kind of study, for "like attracts like" in the dynamics of the inner worlds, which implicitly calls for high moral standards in any intending magical practitioner.

Nervous sensitivity or over-impressionability is another negative condition that may be a simple lack of spiritual will, social responsibility, or self-respect, possibly exacerbated by ill administered hypnosis or the influence of drugs.

If any imaginative figure appears unacceptable, for whatever reason, it can be made to transform to more congenial form. We are, after all, unless neurotic or pathological, masters of our own interior theatre. It is our own creative imagination that we are using as a magic mirror and we should be well able to control how it responds to inner or outer stimuli.

If, for whatever reason, we cannot so control it, then magical study and practice is best left alone, at least temporarily. The cure for most psychic problems lies not in exorcisms or protective talismans, which tend simply to feed the self-induced delusions by granting them importance and reality, but in grounding our attention and faculties into things of the physical world. Thus the best antidote to any problems of an over stimulated imagination is a good meal, a hot drink, and diverting company or entertainment; or for those of a more Spartan turn of mind, hard mental and physical activity and a cold shower!

Most contacts and images, let it be said, being of the higher worlds, will be constructive, beauteous and healing. We are, after all, seeking and dealing with symbols of growth and enlightenment. Let those who seek baser goals think seriously about who or what they may be contacting, and what the motives of their intended playmates are likely to be.

Magical Images and the Magical Imagination

What we meet when we persist with good intent in magical work is, however, genuine friendship and guidance from inner levels that help us with the living of life in a rewarding and constructive manner. The path is not without its challenges, but the forces we contact will be working within the orbit of divine intelligence, and so all progress will be that of spiritual growth. Heavier challenges may be vouchsafed us at a more advanced level of our studies, but we shall by then be well able to cope with them, and no one is pushed beyond their capabilities.

The means by which such instruction will come to us is through a whole range of magical imagery, so we will examine each type of magical image in turn, to see what type of guidance and instruction we are likely to receive from it.

Chapter 2

Cosmic Charts and Maps

Cosmic Charts or Maps are not so much magical images in themselves as systems of magical images. They are means whereby individual symbols or magical images may be interrelated. With their help we can see the general outline of where we are at, whence we have come, and where we are going.

One of the most important of these cosmic schemes is shown in Figure 2.1. Here we see the Earth placed at the center of the universe. The Earth itself is made up of the traditional elements of Earth and Water, surrounded by an envelope of Air, beyond which is a sphere of Fire. Then come the Heavens, which are in the form of a series of crystalline spheres, each one associated with one of heavenly bodies visible to the naked eye, that appear to pursue a wandering path through the sky. Their order is Moon, Mercury, Venus, Sun, Mars, Jupiter and Saturn.

Beyond these seven spheres is one that contains the fixed stars. These include not only the twelve constellations whose magical images are the signs of the zodiac, but a further thirty-six, for there were forty-eight constellations recognized by astronomers of the ancient world to have a symbolic or magical resonance (The other constellations listed today are comparatively modern additions, based upon the intellectual fancy of seventeenth or eighteenth century astronomers, and not the fruit of the all impor-

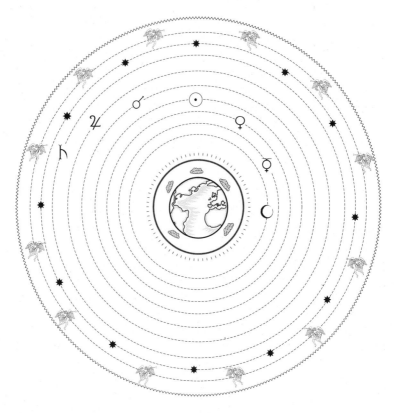

Figure 2.1

The Crystalline Spheres

tant Secondary Imagination). A tenth crystalline sphere beyond all the others is known as the Primum Mobile and is regarded as the sphere of the angels. Traditionally there are nine orders of angels but the ones particularly associated with the Primum Mobile are those who cause all the crystalline spheres to turn. These angels are thus the prime movers of all life and action in the universe.

And beyond this great construct of crystalline spheres, surrounding all, is the Empyreum. This is a state of being beyond all the Heavens which is the source of them all, the Fount of Creation.

Most of this great system of imagery comes down to us from the ancient Greek philosopher Aristotle, who collected together many of the scientific and philosophical ideas of his time. Much of it was lost when the Roman empire fell to the barbarian hordes, but it was later restored by medieval scholars, and in particular by St. Thomas Aquinas.

There was some resistance to this at the time, because some conservative theologians, particularly at the University of Paris, deemed it pagan knowledge, not sanctioned by Biblical authority. Nonetheless it was largely accepted as a useful system and served as the framework of one of the greatest works of world literature, Dante's *Divine Comedy*.

It came in for further criticism in Renaissance times, when it began to be realized that this system of imagery was not a true representation of the physical universe. Thus in 1543 the mathematician Copernicus tried placing the Sun at the center of our planetary system, and later scientific astronomical observation confirmed his theory to be true, despite strong rearguard action by church authorities, as in their celebrated attempt to muzzle Galileo.

This completely exploded the old Aristotelian system as a valid description of the physical universe, but what the Copernican revolutionaries and their successors, the modern materialists, failed to realize is that it remains a very useful description of the spiritual and praeter-natural universe of which the physical universe is but a shell.

For in magical and spiritual terms, not only the Earth, but each individual upon it, is a center of the universe. And this is because each individual perspective of the universe is unique and as valid as any other. Thus, from the collective standpoint of humanity, the Earth remains at the center of the system. So when it comes to experience of the inner worlds, the old system still holds good, and provides channels of imagery through which psychic and spiritual force will flow.

We do not have to accept this as a dogmatic principle, for we can try it out for ourselves. Let us use it as our first practical example of the use of magical imagery. And although we cannot guarantee results or instant success for everybody, the exercise we give has proved effective for a number of students of widely differing backgrounds.

Invocation of the Spheres

Be still within your room and form a dedicated center. If there is a group of you, sit in a circle around a candle or sanctuary light. If you are alone, or if there are only two or three of you, imagine you form part of a circle of like-minded souls who seek to aid you in your work. It does not matter if you do not recognize your invisible co-workers. Simply be aware of them in faith.

Be conscious of the world of nature outside your room: of the trees, the plants, the flowers, the small animals, and the elemental beings that organize their forces. Be aware, if you will, of the great being of the Earth, Gaea herself, within her body of earth and sea.

Be aware of her breathing: of the air enclosing the surface of the Earth; the movement of the winds across the landscapes and the oceans; the rise of water into the air through the warmth of the Sun, and its precipitation again as dew, rain or snow. See the clouds in the skies as changing expressions upon the face of nature.

Cosmic Charts and Maps

And at the limits of the atmosphere see an encircling sphere of protective light. This has sometimes been called a ring of inner fire. It is the spiritual counterpart of what is called the ozone layer. It withholds and protects the beings of the Earth in many unsuspected ways.

Now imagine a sphere of crystal whose extent about the Earth is as high as the Moon. You may imagine the figure of the Moon upon its sphere, if you will, but there is no need to visualize more. Simply be aware that the crystal sphere itself represents the tuned consciousness of an order of angels that beams down strength and constancy to humankind and all that live and move and have their being upon the planet.

There is no need to dwell long in this realization once the initial effort is made. Extend your visualizing powers to another crystal sphere whose bounds extend to the distance of Mercury. Be aware of this as the focussed consciousness of angels of intelligence and communication, bringing intellectual light to the denizens of the Earth below.

Now extend your vision to another crystal sphere, one that coincides with the orbit of Venus. It represents and radiates love and beauty to all below.

Pass on to visualize a further sphere, this one radiant with the Sun's light, and as high as the Sun. It beams down, like the rays of the Sun, health, harmony, light and life-giving power to the Earth within its care.

Next see a crystalline sphere that coincides with the orbit of Mars, the focus of angelic beings of truth and right and justice.

Beyond this one, visualize the sphere that corresponds to the orbit of Jupiter and mediates the angelic influence of order and benign rulership.

Magical Images and the Magical Imagination

And then imagine the crystal sphere that has at its limits far-off Saturn, and mediates the principles of organization in form and the upholding of the necessary laws of nature.

Beyond this sphere is one that has engraved upon it, as on a crystal decanter, all the stars of the heavens visible to the human eye from Earth. These are the star angels whose influences pour in from the constellations. Not only those of the zodiac but of the other great asterisms such as the Pleiades and the Great Bear, and brilliant individual stars such as Sirius, Polaris, Regulus, or Vega, that beam down a plethora of spiritual influences that are necessary for the well-being of the Earth.

And then beyond this is the outermost sphere of all, of complete clarity. It is the sphere of the holy angels themselves, sometimes called the Primum Mobile, that keeps all the cycles of being moving, be they cycles of time or cycles of space, of birth and growth and death, of individuals or of nations. And if you listen carefully, you may hear the angels singing; it is what has sometimes been called the harmony of the spheres — not only the harmony of the working of a beautiful organism, but also a paean of praise for the Creative Spirit beyond who conceived it.

Our consciousness is not capable of penetrating beyond the outer sphere, even in symbolic vision. But a reflection of what lies beyond can come to our awareness. As an expression in sight and substance of the harmony of the spheres, see a holy rain begin to fall. It is as delicate as newly forming dew, like the lightest of light mists. And it falls gently but inexorably through all the spheres. See it pass through each and every one until it falls upon the Earth outside your room and brings a freshness and a new-washed feeling to all that is within.

Cosmic Charts and Maps

And as you become aware of this you may see, in your midst, at the center of your circle (which is also the center of all the crystal spheres, and whose ultimate circumference is beyond them all in the Uncreate Reality), a growing radiance. You may see, or be otherwise aware of, no more than a sense of love and light, although many have seen standing in the center a child, the Son of Light, the Ever-living Young One, radiating peace and seeking personal and individual contact with each and every one, head to head, heart to heart, and feet to feet, as signifying the Way.

If you can, be aware of and reciprocate this contact, and seek to mediate it to the world, so that it penetrates all humanity, and influences the actions of your own small life. Now let the vision fade, and return your attention back to the world of your present duties and desires.

*****

This spherical model of the universe of magical images is capable of considerable elaboration. Dante filled his vision with a vast range of ancillary symbolism, including contemporary political events and personalities which, unless we are scholars of fourteenth century Italian history and culture, are not too helpful to most of us today. Nonetheless this great work of medieval literature is an interesting example of how a general Cosmic Chart or Plan can be broken down into various landscapes, which is the next stage for the practical use of magical imagery.

For instance, Dante's cosmic traveller starts in a dark forest, aware of fearsome beasts that may be a threat to him as he tries to make his way towards a green hill in the distance. This turns out to be the start of a very long journey, for after meeting his guide, the poet-magician Virgil, he is led on a path down into the Earth and through

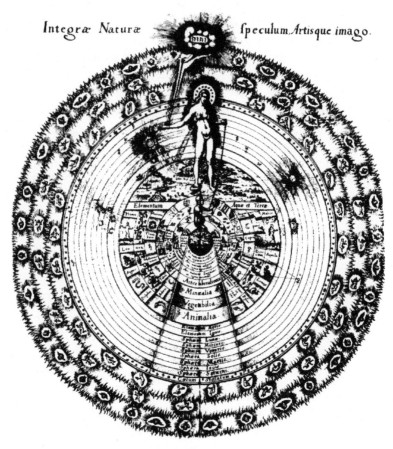

Figure 2.2

The Soul of the World as link between
God and Nature

a series of underworld scenarios that are a reverse pattern of the heavens that we have just described. Passing through the center of the Earth he comes, on the other side of the world, to a mountain whose spiral ascent leads through various ordeals of purgation and tests to the Earthly paradise — the Garden of Eden before the Fall. From there, with the assistance of his ideal lover, Beatrice, and other heavenly guides, he rises through each of the

Crystalline Spheres, meeting their angelic and other denizens, until he emerges into the Empyreum. Here there floats a great white rose, the *rosa mystica*, each of whose petals is made up of spiritual beings, and whose golden center is the seat of the Godhead. Dante's *Divine Comedy* was therefore not only a work of literature but a chart for the examination, cure and ascent of the soul in spiritual self realization.

Nor was it the last use of it in this manner. The most well known illustration of the system, and arguably the best, is the famous engraving by de Bruy for the seventeenth century Rosicrucian Robert Fludd, showing the Soul of the World as link between God and Nature (Figure 2.2).

There are, however, many other ways of depicting these dynamics, and one of the most useful is the Tree of Life of the Qabalah. This is also a series of circles, although not usually set out one within the other, but laid out in a pattern of triangles and squares. That is, there is a network of "paths" connecting the spheres, as in Figure 2.3.

At first sight this may not look much like a tree, but essentially it is a pattern of relationships, and in this sense it is akin to a family tree. However, the interrelationships are not of social alliances but the dynamics that go to make up the structure of any created being. In other words it is a "general systems model" of the principles of creation.

Each circle on the Tree corresponds to one of the crystalline spheres in our previous diagram, and they are in the same order. That is, starting at the top and zigzagging down, in a sequence that is known as the Lightning Flash, they represent the Primum Mobile, the Fixed Stars, Saturn, Jupiter, Mars, the Sun, Venus, Mercury, the Moon and the Earth. There are also three Veils beyond the Primum Mobile — and indeed surrounding the whole Tree — that represent the outer aspects of the Empyreum.

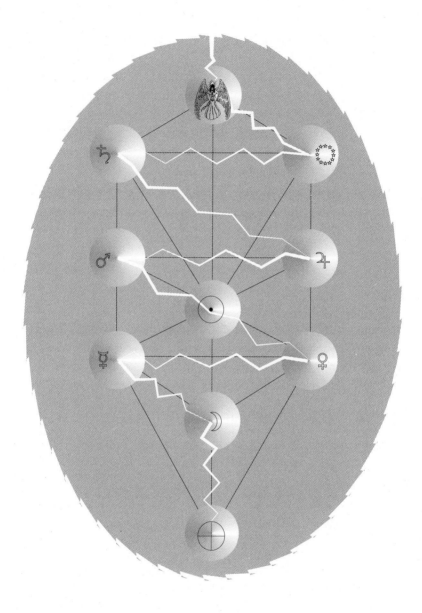

Figure 2.3

The Lightning Flash on the Tree of Life

Cosmic Charts and Maps

The benefit of the pattern of paths between the spheres is that they can themselves be invested with symbolism or magical images, and we can pass by them from one sphere to another, in visualization. The Tree of Life has thus become a major tool of meditational training in the West because it enables us to interrelate a vast compendium of magical images and associated experience.

Each sphere, for example, can be imagined as a temple building, with each path as a journey through a symbolic landscape between them. We shall come to examples of symbolic landscapes later. For the moment it is sufficient to realize that the Tree of Life is a Cosmic Map that enables us to tap into many types and levels of experience. For each circle is not only a crystalline sphere with planetary attributions, it can readily carry a whole host of other applications.

As an illustration of this we can try some practical work with magical images based upon the Tree of Life applied to the aura, although first we will need to say something briefly about the aura that surrounds each and every one of us.

As well as a physical body, we each have more subtle vehicles for our soul to indwell. At its lowest level we can think of this in terms of a kind of electromagnetic cloud that extends a certain way into physical space all around us. This is our personal "atmosphere," although it has more subtle elements to it than the psycho-physical or the electromagnetic. In its subtler aspects it extends a considerable way into what we may come to know as "inner space," and these are of considerable potential power.

We can visualize the aura in various ways, but the simplest is in terms of an ovoid shape, becoming more sphere-like as it extends. It then becomes not unlike the system of crystalline spheres we have been describing. And these spheres have links to different psychological dynamics within us.

Looked at in another way, however, the aura can also be seen to contain a system of power points, and these power points have a certain correspondence with the system of spheres on the Tree of Life.

Remember in all of this, however, that we are dealing with the powers of the imagination, and formulating "magical images." There is no direct link between the images we shall be building and the endocrine glands, or the psycho-physical power points within the etheric vehicle that are known in the East as the chakras.

This is, in one sense, a safety mechanism, for it is possible in advanced yoga techniques, with the aid of certain postures and complex breathing techniques, to work with visualizations and chants that impinge directly upon the etheric body and the autonomic nervous system. This may well be a valid mode of progress for those who can emulate the conditions of an oriental contemplative monk, including close supervision by a personal guru and rigid conditions of diet, life-style and seclusion.

The western methods we advocate do not aim permanently to sensitize the inner faculties, but rather to arouse these powers for a specific short space of time only. This is the prime purpose of group meditation and ceremonial actions or ritual. Here, the play acting or dramatic faculty is used to heighten the Secondary Imagination by the controlled use of symbolic story lines. We can do the same thing by the individual visualization and intelligent use of magical images.

This being clearly understood, we can start to build up a framework of personal magical images based loosely upon the cosmic charts of Crystalline Spheres and Tree of Life, and these can be usefully and safely related to the dynamics of our own aura.

First let us take into account the basic polarity of spirit and matter. Within the make-up of the human being this is represented by the Divine Spark and the Physical Body. In terms of magical images within the aura, each can be seen as a power point visualized as a disc of light. One just above the head, which represents our individual spiritual principle. The other just beneath our feet, which represents the pattern of our life on Earth.

Midway between these two points, on the physical level, we have a muscular wall within our torso, called the diaphragm. This plays a major role in our breathing, in the essential process that keeps our body functioning from minute to minute. The diaphragm, although a physical organ, represents an important inner division within our aura.

Above it are the heart and the lungs, concerned with the intake and expulsion of life giving air, and the circulation round the body of its carrier, the blood. Below it is a massive nervous center called the solar plexus, and the stomach and other organs concerned with the intake and processing of food to fuel the fires of the body.

We can now formulate the basic spiritual and material poles within our aura, and an operational midpoint between them.

A disc of diamond light above our head, which represents the fount of our spiritual integrity; that spark of divinity, or divine impress, which makes each one of us unique as an individual human being.

Another disc beneath our feet, which we can imagine ourselves standing upon, or which our feet rest upon if we choose to take up the other best position for practicing western meditation, a poised sitting position with the spine straight, and the hands resting upon the tops of the thighs, which are horizontal with the ground (with the assistance of a small foot stool, if necessary).

This disc can be seen in the traditional colors of Earth, which are fourfold: quarters of citrine, olive, russet and black, the type of colors often associated with the autumn, or that color the skin of certain apples. This represents our earthly expression. Our fate, our destiny, our path through life, and how well integrated we are with the physical world about us.

Between the two, as a kind of large circular breastplate we can visualize the midpoint disk, like a great sun of gold. This combines two auric centers. The heart, which is associated with our higher ideals, our aspirations, our feelings of personal vocation or destiny. And the solar plexus, which links us in fellow feeling with others, either in personal friendship or emotional ties with family or loved ones, and in a more general sense, of team spirit, loyalty or other types of enthusiasm.

There are two further discs we may now take into account — two centers of creative expression.

The higher one we can visualize before the throat as a lavender colored disc. The throat contains the organ of speech; that which above all distinguishes us as creative and highly communicative beings above the level of the "dumb beasts."

The lower creative center we share with all the animal creation, and it is represented by a deep purple disc before our organs of generation, which above all physical characteristics differentiate us in gender, and are the fount not only of biological creativity but of the libidinous drive that lies behind much physical action and ambition.

as the out-breath, with a similar pause between each inhalation and exhalation. A slow mental count of four can be a useful guide to begin with. This should be done in as normal and comfortable way as possible; do not breath excessively deeply as this may lead to hyperventilation, causing dizziness and loss of the gentle self-control of your faculties that we are seeking.

Now be aware of a point of bright diamond light above your head. You may, after a while, physically begin to feel it, as an actual sensitivity at the top of your scalp, but do not strive unduly for this. All of us as individuals have our own way of registering these centers within the auric envelope and secondary phenomena like this, or the lack of them, are not necessarily indicators of progress.

This becoming aware of your own spiritual point just above the head (rather after the fashion of a personal halo) is a valuable exercise in itself, and can be usefully and harmlessly practised at any time of day in convenient circumstances.

Now turn your attention to a point just beneath your feet, as if you were standing upon a disc. You can visualize this as if it were a golden Maltese cross upon a black ground. Again, you may find a certain very slight tingling sensation beneath your feet when you have performed this for some little time. This is a natural feeling of etheric sensitivity that some people may get, and once again, should not be consciously striven for. It is a minor natural effect, not a supernatural phenomenon to be blown up out of all proportion.

The real and important effect of building of these two centers in the aura should be in grounding you spiritually in your daily life. And in one sense it is a kind of wordless prayer to your own spiritual being — or your holy guardian angel, if you like.

Magical Images and the Magical Imagination

You can take your time over this, building up just the two points before you go on to construct any more of the Tree in your aura. One step at a time will bring more effective and lasting results. But when you feel ready you can pass to the next stage, which is to visualize a great golden disc, like the sun, over your diaphragm, so that if it were physical, it would be like a circular breast plate, covering your lower chest and upper abdomen.

You may feel quite a warm glow of love and well being from this exercise. And as you grow more accustomed to it you can try to feel and to separate out those feelings which seem to pertain more to your heart (that is, above the diaphragm), and those which pertain more to the solar plexus, just below the diaphragm.

In esoteric terms you will be beginning to differentiate between two of the Spiritual Alchemical Elements — that of Air above the diaphragm, and that of Water below. This has its physical correspondences in that above the diaphragm we have the lungs, the organs of breath, and below the diaphragm the digestive organs with their largely liquid related functions. It follows that the center above the head corresponds to the Alchemical Element of Fire, (Spiritual Fire and the Divine Spark), and that below the feet to Alchemical Earth. When we have all four in balanced function we are on the way to expressing the Quintessence, which is our full human capability, greater than the sum of its parts.

Having well established this center of our being we can pass to the remaining two centers, and you can build these two together, for they relate closely to one another in function, although at different levels. You can formulate them as slightly smaller discs than the golden central one. A disk of a beautiful lavender color, just before your throat; that is, at the topmost point of your torso. And a similar disk of a deep purple before your generative organs, before the lowermost point of your torso. You may find it helpful to elaborate this symbolism slightly by seeing a silver star in the higher lavender disc, and a crescent moon, (points up), in a purple sky in the lower.

We have now formulated the Sephiroth of the Middle Pillar of the Tree of Life within the aura, and the benefits of this should soon become evident in greater poise and inner equilibrium. To this may be added the side Pillars. You may best visualize these as if you were standing between them. See and "feel" a dark pillar to your right and a bright pillar to your left. This should give a further sense of well grounded balance and stability. Upon each pillar you can then imagine, when you are ready, three further discs.

It may be best to build these in pairs, at any rate in the first instance. At a level with your head, be aware in the right hand pillar of a dark, almost black sphere, and upon the left hand pillar one of bright silver, almost like a mirror. These represent quite high intuitive or mental functions of which you may not hitherto have been very aware within yourself. But this form of visualization will in the course of time start to bring this kind of awareness about, in the form of flashes of intuition or inspiration or clear sightedness.

It is not easy to make an intellectual definition of the difference between these two topmost pillar points, because their functions are above that of our normal intellectual consciousness. It must suffice to say that the silver is like the intuitive receptivity to the highest spiritual wisdom, and the black is like a dark womb of understanding, particularly of the application of uncreate realities into the restriction of form expression and consciousness. More, we cannot usefully say at this point.

At the next level, corresponding more or less to shoulder height, you can become aware of two discs representing two sides of yourself, that might be summed up as what you are and what you do. On your right side see, therefore, a disc of flaming reds that indicates yourself in action, going and getting and doing. And balancing this upon your left side, a disc of deep blue indicates yourself in calmness and wisdom taking full account of your own strengths and weaknesses and the needs and demands of the moment before embarking upon any action. You can, given sufficient practice, utilize these two discs quite actively in daily life. Concentrating upon the red one when action and initiative are called for, and the blue one when you need to hold back and assess a situation carefully before committing yourself to an action you might later regret.

Finally, we come to the discs at about hip level upon the side pillars. To the right you can build an orange disc which represents the right control of your mind and intellect and to the left one of green that represents right expression of your emotions. Again concentration upon these when you need to use your wits when facing an intellectual problem, or to keep the right level of expression or control in an emotional situation, are practical applications of this particular exercise.

******

We have now examined and gained some practical experience of a couple of Cosmic Maps or Charts. There are, it should be said, a number of others from which we could have chosen. In the East, for example, apart from the detailed yoga practices, a similar all inclusive system is to be found in the imagery of Mount Meru. This is a fabulous island which compromises the whole universe, with its hells of hungry ghosts and assorted demons below, and upon its peak a city of the gods and above that a series of heavens; whilst all around is a great ocean with mighty islands and an all encompassing ring of cosmic mountains.

Other, more abstract, systems exist, such as the Enneagram; a system of nine points round a circle, which has a mathematical basis and derives from Sufi mysticism. It is much favored by followers of the spiritual teachers Gurdjieff and Ouspensky and has also been developed as a psycho-therapeutic device by some groups within the Roman Catholic church.

However, it does not serve our purpose to make a comprehensive collection of systems, which would call for a work of encyclopedic proportions, and only increase our intellectual knowledge rather than our wisdom and understanding. The ability to work confidently in one or two systems is of more use and benefit than a superficial knowledge of many.

And although some of these systems may appear to differ quite fundamentally in their outer appearance, they do have an underlying unity. This is because they are describing the same basic principles but are simply using a different symbolic language, or system of magical images, to do so.

Magical Images and the Magical Imagination

Chapter 3

Landscapes and Journeys

Whatever Cosmic Map we choose will help us to understand how the inner world is structured. In this sense a Cosmic Map is a comprehensive magical image in its own right. If we identify with it and build it as a pattern within our own aura it helps us to maintain personal balance and gain general understanding of our own spiritual potential.

However, it will also reveal more if we examine and experience it in its detailed parts. By moving from one part of the system to another, we will find ourselves embarking upon a quest, or initiatory journey. The overall Cosmic Map becomes, therefore, a ground plan for a number of possible journeys through ordered states of consciousness.

In practical terms, any journey must take place through some kind of landscape. So the next stage of our practical work with magical images is to use them in a linear way that will take us through an initiatory journey or story.

Such journeys are common in all myth and legend. There are stories of adventure, of quests, of pilgrimage, of exploration, of rescue, of conquest. Any story has some kind of initiatory potential. That is what makes story telling so popular throughout the ages. Some stories may have more numinous content than others but even the most banal tale can have its resonances with deeper journeyings within and beyond the soul.

Magical Images and the Magical Imagination

We have already mentioned Dante and his long journey through the underworld to a mountain of purification and his subsequent ascent into the heavens. This is an example of a Cosmic Map being used quite directly as a system of landscapes for visionary travel.

However a multitude of others exists. Some are plainly allegorical and piously explicit as Bunyan's *Pilgrim's Progress*. Others may be scatological and hilarious adventures, as Apuleius' *Golden Ass*, which conceals some of the mysteries of the Graeco-Roman cult of Isis. The ancient Greeks had their quest of the Golden Fleece by a band of heroes. And in later times an amalgam of Celtic mythology, British prehistory and Cistercian and Near Eastern mysticism provides us with the Arthurian knights and their various quests including that of the Holy Grail.

These mythological and legendary sources tend to be quite compendious and too long drawn out for practical use in their entirety. Although their value as stories to be read and contemplated at leisure is by no means diminished.

What we seek in our process of "tuning consciousness" is, however, something a little more specific than the whole sweep of an epic or volume of tales. And there is nothing to stop us selecting the bits that we need from the vast rich treasure store of myth, legend and religious tradition.

Whatever the source or background of the magical journeys we choose to make, there are various key scenarios that are particularly apt to the tuning of consciousness. We may list a few examples:

   a) a desert journey towards a temple in the
      wilderness;
   b) a pilgrimage along an ancient track toward a
      sacred circle or mound;
   c) a boat journey down a river to a sacred city or
      island;

d) a sea voyage to a mysterious island or sacred shore;

e) an underground passage to chambers deep within the Earth;

f) the ascent of a winding stairway in a mysterious tower to a chapel or observation point;

g) an aerial journey by chariot and flying horse or other means to a temple in the sky or among the stars.

The detail can be taken from any existing fictional or historical writings, adapted to choice, the main criterion being the evocative stimulation of the imagination. Accomplished and imaginative practitioners will be able to write their own, either prepared in advance for reading, or extemporaneously expressed at the time of working. However, as beginners, we are likely to need the support of external sources and pre-preparation.

In its basic and most elementary format the tuning of consciousness through an imaginary journey may be used as a preparation for magical work. In this function it is commonly called a *Composition of Mood* or *Composition of Place*. In fact the imagery of the imagined place induces the required mood (an elementary pre-tuning of consciousness onto more or less the right wavelength) and in turn, the induced mood aids in forming subsequent spontaneous imagery.

Let us take an example. In order to cover as many aspects as possible within a short compass we will make it a journey that leads from the temple of our own being, into an inner objective world that is experienced first as an ancient trackway through open country that leads to a tower in which inner objective states may be experienced at various levels.

Magical Images and the Magical Imagination

We will choose a symbolic landscape that is likely to appeal to a majority of students: the traditional countryside of old England around Glastonbury, broadly associated with the Arthurian and Holy Grail legends.

Composition of Mood: The Path to the Tower

Being seated comfortably in your meditation position, free from likelihood of disturbance, calm and compose yourself with a minute or two of regular relaxed breathing, and proceed with the formulation of light within the aura as described in the previous chapter.

Now open your inner eyes to the realm of creative visualization, and feel yourself standing upon a disk quartered in the traditional colors of the Earth: citrine, olive, russet and black, which slowly disappears as you find that you are standing upon a hill top in open countryside. A light breeze fans your face, the warmth of the sun high in the heavens is upon your body. Hear the bird song in the trees and hedges, and smell the scent of spring flowers. Beneath your feet is a rough trackway, its natural chalk surface rutted with the passage of flocks and herds and horse and cart traffic through the centuries. And also of pilgrims, for this is an ancient trackway across the Land of Logres, the legendary country of King Arthur, Merlin, the Lady of the Lake, the Grail Castle, and many another sacred and ancient mystery.

The track takes a wandering course across the hills and along with your companions of the way, you follow this ancient way of pilgrimage. It is a pilgrimage towards the holiest earth in Logres, to Glastonbury, the meeting point of many sacred traditions, some of them older than recorded time, some even older than time itself.

Landscapes and Journeys

The trackway leads over the last of the hills, a long low mound that is like a sleeping beast, and is called by the locals Wearyall. Upon its furthest slope you pause to stand beside a thorn tree. This is by tradition the holy thorn where Joseph of Arimathea planted his staff which then miraculously blossomed. To the west can be seen the glint of waves on the distant sea, across the salt marshes. But your eyes are turned across the valley that lies before you, of monastic buildings and villagers' huts, of wattle and daub, to two hills upon the opposite side. One is the emerald green round swell of Chalice Hill, at whose foot lies a holy well. And rising high beside it the pyramid like shape of Glastonbury Tor, with a spiral path around it leading up to a lone tower.

You pass swiftly down the side of Wearyall Hill and through the low lying ground that lies between until you reach the foot of the Tor. Here you scramble up a short steep path to reach the foot of the spiral way. Beside a stile where the spiral path commences, you find a figure gowned in white, a guardian of the Tor, one of the Watchers of Avalon, who has guarded, loved and prayed in this place over the long ages.

*****

This little journey will suffice us for the moment. We can usefully break off here without becoming committed further. And we will take up our journey again a little later.

We have effectively conducted a short Composition of Mood, or Composition of Place, in which we have tuned our consciousness to a particular wavelength or inner dynamic. We can now either proceed or withdraw consciousness back to the physical world. This can be done by retracing our steps in imagination back to the place whence we started and return by that route to our own hearth and home. Such a return procedure need not be long drawn out. Some people prefer to unwind more quickly or more slowly from inner consciousness and retracing the path, either slowly or at speed is an effective way of doing this.

However, it is also possible to return to outer consciousness more quickly still, simply by affirming the will to do so. And indeed in the hopefully rare case of physical interruption of a meditation, this may be a necessity. This can be a bit of a shock however, particularly if we are deeply in to inner consciousness, or if we are of a more sensitive than average disposition. But apart from this minor discomfort there is no need to feel open to dangers about letting inner forces into your outer consciousness in an uncontrolled fashion. There is much needless fear about this, or of the dangers of getting "stuck" if one does not meticulously retrace every step of the way. This is a result of taking the sensible precautions often built in to elementary training procedures a little too seriously. It is always better of course to err on the side of caution but this does not mean that we have to have two belts and three pairs of braces to hold our trousers up.

Having been spiritually centered to begin with in your visualization, after the manner we have described, you are always in control. And even if pulled back suddenly from a very deep inner experience you can always affirm the proper boundary between worlds by means of a simple ritual gesture, such as stamping your foot or clapping your hands, or making a sign of closing curtains, followed by a warm drink or light snack. This is perfectly adequate for any person of normal balance and sensitivity. There is no need to be the psychic equivalent of James Thurber's aunt who worried about electricity leaking into the house if there were no electric light bulb in the socket. Once you have switched off your mental radio receiver you will not continue to hear the program.

Let us take stock of what we have actually been doing. We have started on an imaginative journey that consists of visualizing, in linear sequence, a selection of numinous symbols or magical images.

We began by stimulating our spiritual consciousness and psychic and intuitive sensitivity by a simple exercise of channelling light within the aura. This done, we evoked a pleasant country scene, with an ambience of ancient traditions and aspirations to quest or pilgrimage. This slowly crystallized into a specific location, which in this case was Glastonbury Tor, which is a sacred site of some power in its own right, with both pagan and Christian associations.

It helps to use sites of this type, particularly if you have had the opportunity to visit them physically at some time in the past. A previous visit not only sharpens up your visualizing ability with regard to that particular place, but also forms a subtle etheric link with part of your own aura. This can be more effective than performing rites or meditations at the actual physical site, where satisfactory conditions and freedom from interruption can seldom be guaranteed. In other words, it can prove more effective to make the etheric link with a simple visit, as any tourist, and then to re-evoke the inner dynamics in the controlled conditions of your own temple or own home.

You can also take liberties with an inner landscape and improve slightly upon nature, which is a time honored method in any branch of art. Thus we commenced the journey upon a real ancient trackway, the Ridgeway, which although in physical fact passes a number of ancient sites such as the Uffington White Horse and the Avebury megalithic complex, is not geographically associated with Glastonbury. However, its inner resonances are those of any ancient trackway, and could be readily utilized in this instance.

However, it is not essential to have actually visited any of these physical sites to perform effective work. They can indeed be entirely fictional. The main criterion is that they move us emotionally, in however slight a way. It is that slight movement of emotion that provides the initial power for our working with the images. It is a form of priming the pump. Later, as our work progresses, the images will begin to feed back a power of there own. We then have "lift off."

And so let us now resume our journey. Having broken off it may be best for you to start again at the very beginning and work your way through to the point we have reached. For those with a little more experience in these matters it may be possible effectively to take up immediately where we left off. There is no such thing as an outer time lapse upon the inner planes. However, remember in all of this that, as in all acquirement of a natural skill, it is better to "make haste slowly." In other words, do not skimp on the five finger exercises if you really want eventually to play the magical keyboard well.

In the continued journey that follows we shall find that there can be journeys through interior locations as well as through landscapes, and also that we may meet with figures of people or other beings on the way. For the moment we will simply take these as they come, without too much dalliance, until we have gained some experience of dealing with inanimate magical images. The more complex issues surrounding our possible relationship with animate images will find their place later.

The Journey to the Tower (continued)

For the moment we simply take note of the Watcher of Avalon who stands at the start of the spiral path that leads up and around the Tor.

44

Landscapes and Journeys

We clamber over the stile, assisted by the robed figure, who at the same time takes the opportunity to scrutinise us deeply with a penetrating gaze.

Once over, we start up the steep track, worn in the chalk, that takes us up in a clockwise direction around the conical hill. We are aware, as we climb, of the strength of elemental life about us, in the grass and wild flowers, cropped by the grazing cattle through which we pass. We are conscious of the sweep of the Somerset levels as we pass ever higher upward, marshes that some short while ago were under the sea, when the Tor and its surrounding hills were islands, and now cut with the straight gleaming lines of "rhines" or drainage ditches.

Finally, somewhat breathless, we arrive at the top of the Tor, and there standing before us is a tower. However, it is not the bare and broken down tower that is visible upon the physical plane, the remains of a demolished church, but an altogether grander edifice, an inner tower known only to those with the power of vision.

The door to the tower is set high up above the ground. This signifies that none who are unworthy are allowed to enter in, but by virtue of our dedication we find we are expected, and a wooden ramp materializes in the air, leading from before our feet to the door itself. And feeling an ambience of welcome from the invisible guardians, we are allowed to pass across.

Our feet ring hollowly upon the boards, and at the top, at the narrow wooden doorway, we are greeted by a fair maiden, who, with many willing hands to help her, takes our travel stained outer clothes, and places us at our ease.

The large circular room is warm and bright. An open fire roars in a great fireplace against the wall before us. The atmosphere is one of a welcoming home, with love and peace and gentleness pervading all. It is here we may also meet with friends from outer life, or with loved ones, be they in or out of physical life. For this is the place of the center of the heart's desire, the true hearth of every home, and its fire is the central fire for every family hearth. We may refresh ourselves within its atmosphere and take some essence of it back to our own homes in the outer world when we depart. The maiden, who is the tender of the hearth, tells you that you will always be made welcome here.

We are also conscious, after a while, of levels of the tower that lie beneath us. And as we start to think about this a door bursts open, and standing within the portal is a great strong man, in appearance like a blacksmith. He has curling chestnut colored hair and rippling muscles and smiles broadly. He wears a leather apron and bears the hammer and tongs of a smith. We see that he stands at the top of a stairway leading downwards, and he beckons and invites us to see what is there.

We descend a spiral stair that is as narrow and tightly turning as that within a mill, and as we reach the bottom pass into another warm and welcoming room. We find we are standing on a rough stone and earthen floor. The whole place is like a cellar, lit with a ruddy glow from fires, some of which heat an oven, from whence there comes the fragrant smell of new-baked bread. There are also stills against other parts of the walls, some fermenting wine and other strange liquors and herbal essences.

We can see that animals are stalled here, for there are secret gates that lead out through the hillside to their pasturage. We also see the sleek coats of horses, along with the duller coats of cattle in to be milked. In another part of the cellar stands a blacksmith's forge and anvil for the making of tools and weapons. There also appears to be a kiln for making pottery. The mighty smith looks on all around him with pride and is pleased that we are impressed with the diversity of his crafts.

Then he places his finger to his lips, and points to a dark corner we had not noticed before, and we see that he is indicating a trap door set in the floor. We look at it, wondering where it might lead, and as we do so, become aware of a figure who moves forward from the shadows beyond it.

He is an old man, with a long white beard, holding a staff. Suddenly he produces from beneath his dark grey cloak a lighted lantern, which he fixes to the top of his staff. Then, with surprising agility, he bends forward and throws open the trap door.

We see a flight of rough stone steps leading downwards into the earth. With a glint in his eye that could be either of warning or of humor, he raises his lantern aloft, and proceeds down the stairway, indicating that we should follow.

We pass down a dark and steeply descending stairway, conscious only of the bare earth ceiling and walls about us, and the dim light going before, ever downward. We also feel that we are observed, but by whom or what we cannot imagine.

At last the downward journey ends, and we find ourselves in an underground cavern. As our eyes grow accustomed to the dark, lit only by the old man's lantern, we see that we are in a crypt. On ledges and crevices in small antechambers and passage ways are coffins. But there is no atmosphere of decay or death or neglect, but rather of a living ancient wisdom, as of memories and dreams from remote ages. We feel a sense of kinship with all that is held within this place. We are in the presence of a sort of sleeping treasure house of human experience.

This is the place of the ancestors. Our own ancestors, of our own blood line or of other races who have inhabited the land of our birth.

Magical Images and the Magical Imagination

We are conscious of the sound of the flowing of underground waters. And by listening to this soft background murmur we find it can be a vehicle to tune in to the thoughts and dreams of those who have gone before on life's way, whose lands we share and inherit, or through whose veins there ran the same blood that courses through our own. And from this place we can receive love, strength and advice of an enduring and earthly wise nature. Here is the source of all family and national tradition; in stories, rhymes, myths and legends. We rest here awhile so that we may recall this ambience when, in times of stress in the outer world, we need the wisdom and strength of the past.

Now the old man indicates that it is time for us to depart, and looking toward the stairway, we find that we have been joined by another guide. This one is also one of our forebears, and yet he also has another guise and function, for he is one of the greater guides and guardians, who helps to guide the destinies and well being of nations. He has a Tudor style of dress, a scholar's cap of that era, and a golden chain around his neck, of linked S shaped devices, from which depends a great seal of office.

He warmly greets us personally, holding our two hands clasped together within his own, before he leads us out of this place. After a salutation of respect and regard for its ancient guardian, he leads us swiftly up the stone stairway, back into the cellars of the tower, where the great smith stands holding a huge tray full of steaming fresh baked loaves, one of which we can take if we desire. We are also conscious, as we pass through this place, of fleeting figures, dimly seen, who belong here but are not of the human kind. They are elemental creatures of the green wood, of field and grove, river and lake, and as we realize their presence the smell of the loam and fragrance of the hedgerow and herb and wild flower comes also to our perception.

Landscapes and Journeys

But we have no time to linger, for the master passes on, up the next spiral stairway, to the room that first we entered. It is full of friendly chatter and laughter and no cross words can be heard. We notice that from the windows can be seen an idyllic countryside. It is the ideal of the Land of Logres, the natural form of the Earthly Paradise as it could be expressed in the mode of the countryside of the Isles of Albion.

*****

Again this is a suitable point where we can pause on our inner journey, in order to review some of the things we have seen and experienced. We have effectively made a small round trip and if we wish can return the way we came, out of the tower, and down the Tor and along the ancient track to our starting point — or more directly if we so prefer, for the actual tower has its location within ourselves. What we have been doing in effect is to approach our own aura objectively from the outside (in imaginative terms) rather than subjectively from the inside.

When we went into the welcoming ambience of the room of the hearth fire it was as if we were becoming objectively conscious of our own solar plexus center. We have made an objective place of it and have gone inside. Most of our journeys are thus within ourselves; within our greater selves, that is to say; within the large ovoid of our aura that stretches all around us into inner space.

And when we then descended the stairs, first into the cellar under the hospitality of the blacksmith, and then into the caverns yet further below, under the invitation and the guidance of the hermit, we were experiencing something of the roots of our own being. These are represented by the lower psychic centers within the aura, corresponding roughly to Yesod and Malkuth upon the Tree of Life, in Qabalistic terms, the welcoming room above having its equivalent in Tiphareth.

It may come as a surprise that in search of spiritual values we should go down rather than up in our journeying through the tower. There are very good reasons for this, and we should also bear in mind that when we started our exercises of light within the aura we commenced at the top, at the crown above the head, and carried the light and the force downwards until it was at our feet.

From here we set out on our magical journey. And on this journey we have simply raised awareness up to the Tiphareth/Solar Plexus level again, when we entered the tower. And this enabled us the better to stabilize and go down to experience the lower dynamics, which normally are beneath the threshold of outer consciousness. This is a visit to the subconscious, or the unconscious if you like, should you prefer to use the more familiar (if implicitly materialist and limiting) definitions of analytical psychology

Furthermore, it is very important to realize that we need to come to terms with these "lower" dynamics, for they are as important spiritually, as any "higher" aspirations. The spiritual quest is not a flight from the problems and conditions of the physical world and our roots within it. It is one that seeks understanding and control of this lower world in which we live and move and have our being.

We are in no fit state to seek direct contact with higher spiritual forces if we have failed to come to terms with them in their expression in everyday life. To seek the higher whilst neglecting the call and the just dues of the lower, is to risk becoming that vague kind of subjective visionary who is out of touch with the practicalities of life and ineffectual in all mundane things.

We have, however, now taken a short magical journey, using images of an interior as well as an exterior landscape, which we have seen it is possible to interpret as part of a Cosmic Map. That is to say in terms of journeys on the Tree of Life up and down the central paths between Tiphareth and Malkuth, the central and the lowest spheres respectively. There is, needless to say, a lot more to the dynamics of what we have seen than this, but we have at least scratched the surface. Further experience building on from this will teach more.

However, we can now pass on to the next type of magical image, which consists of temples, shrines and the artifacts to be found within them.

Magical Images and the Magical Imagination

Chapter 4

Temples and Shrines

*T*here is great variety in the structure of temples and all that goes within them. This includes the dedicated shrines that may form part of the edifice, and the consecrated or symbolic objects to be found there. However every magical temple conforms to the basic underlying pattern of an inner reality, just as every suit of clothes, however stylishly cut, must conform to the basic shape of the human form.

A magical temple is a model of the inner universe at large. Therefore somewhere or somehow within it there is likely to be a representation of the principle of duality. This is not the duality of good and of evil but the opposite poles of polarity (positive/negative, active/passive, force/ form, light/dark, hot/cold) between which the web of life is strung. This is often found in the form of twin pillars, sometimes with an overriding arch, and may be at the door of the temple or at some prominent place within.

There may also be a formal representation of the four-fold principle of the Elements that go to make up the substance of life. These are traditional states of being known as Fire, Air, Water and Earth. At the most physical and obvious level these universal principles are expressed in the four states of matter, plasma, gas, liquid and solid, but there is much more to the Elements than this. They embody basic qualities of expression at every level of manifestation, from the highest spiritual realms to the physical states of matter we have just described.

When expressed at the highest spiritual level they often appear in ancient symbolic forms. Examples from the Bible are the Holy Living Creatures of the Vision of Ezekiel, of Lion, Eagle, Man and Bull, which Christians later applied to the four Evangelists. However, they may be also seen, in slightly varied form, in the signs of the zodiac, the so-called "fixed" signs, of Leo (Fire), Scorpio (Water), Aquarius (Air) and Taurus (Earth), or in the temple statuary of ancient Assyria, the winged lions, winged serpents, winged men and winged bulls.

These are therefore magical images of a particularly ancient and powerful type. However, before we embark upon the complexity of varieties of symbol let us see how the basic principles of duality and the quaternio can be expressed in the simplest possible way. This will be in terms of space. Or how the dedicated space of the temple is laid out. And as they are universal principles they will found to be latent in even the simplest plan.

The basic space could be imagined in the form of a square (or in three dimensions, a cube) conforming to our four-fold Elemental principles, one to each side, plus an over-riding duality of Above and Below at ceiling and floor. But the simplest fundamental form will be a circle, or in three dimensional space, a sphere.

A circle, or a sphere, affirms by its very shape the principle of duality. As a first expression of Unity it has its single source or center, from which every point upon its circumference or surface is equidistant. The primal duality is demonstrated in the complementary principles of the center and the circumference. The center is the focus of centripetal force, and circumference is the expression of centrifugal force.

Temples and Shrines

We may now introduce the Elemental principles by the process of "squaring the circle." That is, we envisage a power point in each of the cardinal directions. So our temple may have an Elemental shrine at East and South and West and North.

It is traditional to divide these into temporal modes, according to the daily and yearly passage of the Sun in northern temperate zones.

Thus East is associated with Dawn and with the Spring;

South is associated with Noon and with Summer;

West is associated with Dusk and with Fall;

North is associated with Midnight and with Winter.

The more esoteric Elemental attributions to the quarters are Air to East; Fire to South; Water to West and Earth to North. And these in turn are associated with traditional "magical weapons," which have their correspondence in the suits of the Tarot pack, and even in the ordinary decks of modern playing cards that derive from them.

Thus East and the Air and the beginnings of things, represented by Dawn and Spring, is associated with the Dagger of Air in the magician's symbolic equipment. This has various adaptations, from the "atheme" of the followers of Wicca, to the sword of the ceremonial magician. Magic was practised by all ranks of medieval society and the difference between witch's dagger and magician's sword is essentially a social and economic one, between villein's cottage and baronial hall. An alternative might be any bladed instrument, and indeed the arrow head, as well as the knife that could be thrown, is particularly appropriate for dedication to Air.

In the South, associated with high summer and with noon, we have the principle of Fire and this is adequately represented by the symbol of the rod or magic wand. Again this can come in various forms from the royal scepter to the broom or staff of the country man or woman. There are some who feel that the sword is more appropriately associated with fire, largely on account of the familiar bellicose quotation of putting something to the fire and the sword, but the rod is the time honored means of controlling and even of carrying fire. We use a rod or poker to control the domestic hearth fire or the celebratory or garden bonfire, and the god Prometheus is said to have brought fire to Earth within a hollow reed — another form of rod.

In the West, associated with evening, and gathering in of the fruits of the Earth we have an appropriate symbol in the receptacle. This again can take many forms, as a chalice, as a drinking horn, and in the communal and culinary form of a cauldron. In the Arthurian legends it may be represented by the Holy Grail, which in fact has no well defined form, appearing in many guises in many situations but always bringing food and drink in material or spiritual form, and the renewal of life. A cup being principally formed to hold a liquid, the appropriate Elemental attribution is Water.

Finally in the North we may have an "earthing" symbol; that which in some way makes sense of the past, confirms the physical present, and contains a plan for the future. This can be in the form of an orb, representing the Earth itself, or the Cosmos or a model of the temple as a whole. It can also appear as some kind of talisman, perhaps a disc of metal inscribed with a sigil of the dedication of the temple, or may be a simple dish containing an offering, and an earthenware dish is as appropriate to the Element of Earth as is one of costly gold or silver.

Temples and Shrines

In the Center of all we may place our center of attention when the four Elements are in balanced equilibrium, that is to say an altar. The simpler this is, probably the better, for it represents the immediate focus of attention, and upon its uncluttered surface can then be placed whatever symbols may be appropriate to the work in hand. However, it is not uncommon, and entirely appropriate, to have some kind of unifying symbol associated with it. And most often this will be a light, sometimes hanging above the surface of the altar, whilst within its recesses may be kept holy relics or dedicated scripts that encapsulate the aspirations of those who use the temple.

From this basic outline very considerable complexity can be laid on. A simple but fruitful form of temple could be elaborated in terms of Tarot images, with the suits of Swords, Wands, Cups and Coins at the four quarters, with the Trumps ready to manifest at the center.

The possibilities are legion, and in the end the personal temple of the magician, if working alone, reflects his or her own understanding of the inner universe. It is a personal three-dimensional Jungian mandala, should one choose to put it in psychological terms. And if it is a temple constructed by a group then it equally expresses the group's aspirations, or at least those of its founders.

To demonstrate some of the principles we have outlined, we can continue our journey through the tower. We do not have to retrace all the steps we have taken into the lower parts of the tower, but on entering the initial room of welcome can go straight up by the spiral stair to the level of the Temple of the Elements led by our Guide to the higher regions, the man in the Tudor scholar's cap and golden chain of office.

The Temple of the Elements

We proceed up the spiral stairway, which has become quite wide at the top and gives on to a door. The door appears to be of cedar or of some similar resinous wood, and there is emblazoned upon it a five-pointed star, point upward. This is a sigil that signifies the Spirit of man in control of and in cohesion with the four Elements.

Our guide knocks upon the door, three measured raps, and the door swings open before us. We are met by a waft of incense, which immediate raises our spirits to the work in hand as we push aside the heavy veil that hangs within the doorway, and pass within.

We find that we have come into a circular room, carpeted with a checkered design of black and white squares, indicative of the basic polarity behind all manifestations of life. Within the center is a small altar, emblematic of unity, upon which there is a single light, upon a candlestick that is in the form of the caduceus of Mercury, that is to say with the two serpents of alternating polarity curled about its slender stem, and a pair of wings just below the flame. The altar itself is a double cube, that is to say, one cube placed upon another, which symbolically represents a figure of ten sides, the number that symbolically represents the Earth. There is a white cloth upon the altar, upon which rests an open book, its illuminated pages shining in the candle's light.

We see that there are four great circular objects at four quarters of the temple, that might well be huge windows, each concealed behind a curtain. That in the East is citrine yellow; that in the South is russet red, that in the West is olive green, and that in the North is black. Each is flanked by two pillars, the right hand one, as we look at it, is silver, the left hand one gold. The tops of the pillars are spherical, the one on the left representing a globe of the earth, with its seas and continents, the one on the right representing the celestial sphere, with its constellations as seen from the earth. Arching above the pillars and joining their tops is the sculptured form of an angel with outstretched wings above and hands upon the spheres. The name of each angel is written on a flying ribbon carved just below them. In the East Raphael, the angel of healing. In the South Michael, the protective warrior angel who stands in the sun. In the West Gabriel, the divine messenger. And in the North Auriel, the angel of light, the light of the stars of the night sky.

The door through which we have entered is no longer to be seen, being behind the ring of golden curtains, but our Guide stands there as guardian to mark its place. There is sufficient light from the central candle for us to see all clearly. And in the ceiling above the altar is another sculpted angelic form, whose wings spread widely above us, along with a ribbon containing his name, Sandalphon, the presiding angel over this temple of the Earth and of the Four Elements.

In that which follows, visualize yourself as doing the actions described — not as if you are standing outside yourself as an observer, but as if you are within your own body performing what is described. As a preliminary, imagine the feel of ceremonial robes about you. An inner robe of white, representing purity of intention, secured by a girdle of three stranded rope, one strand of purple, one of orange and one of green, that signifies the need for a three fold approach to the Mysteries of Earth, one of mystical devotion, one of magical knowledge, and one of elemental power.

Upon your feet are red shoes, representing the power to walk upon the higher planes. Upon your breast, pendant from a golden ribbon about your neck is a silver talisman, a disc that bears upon it a motto, chosen by yourself, representing your aspiration in your pursuit of higher knowledge and power. About your shoulders is a rich and heavy outer robe of gold, and upon your head a crown, that consists of a light golden band about your brow set with twelve gems, representing the signs of the zodiac, and at the apex of four arcs of gold arching up, a diamond above the crown of your head.

Now go to stand in imagination immediately at the western side of the central altar, facing eastward, and perform what is known as the Qabalistic Cross. That is to say, trace out in the air, with your right hand, first of all a point above your head, looking up towards the hovering angel above, as you do so, and then sweep your hand and arm down to indicate a spot beneath your feet, feeling as you do so, the power of the presiding angel of the temple striking down into the earth below, and empowering with potential divine power the whole of the temple. Bring your hand back to your heart and then complete a form of the cross first to the right and then to the left, in an invocation of the powers of the pillars of equilibrium before clasping your hands before your heart and the sigil with your name of aspiration that hangs between your hands and your heart.

After a pause to take all this in, proceed slowly to the eastern quarter of the temple, before the citrine yellow curtains. Make the sign of a pentagram in the air before you, starting at the top, being conscious of the quarter's angel towards which you point and invoking his power and blessing as you do so, then swing your pointing hand down to lower left, up to upper right, straight across to upper left, down to lower right, and then back up to the top again. You may now intone the name of the angel Raphael physically if you wish (pronounced Rah-phah-el). When intoning in this manner physically, take a deep breath, and expel the air slowly by an upward movement of the dia-

phragm, letting the sound resonate in your head cavities as you do so. Relaxation is the key to success in this matter of "vibrating" divine names.

Now, standing before the two pillars imagine yourself taking hold of the center of the curtains that hang between them, sweeping them back with an outward movement of your arms and step forward to stand immediately between the pillars of the East. You can, if you wish, vibrate the Qabalistic Holy Name of God associated with this quarter, as you stand there. This is the four letters of the name IHVH (pronounced Yohd-Heh-Vow-Heh).

As soon as you open the curtains, a bright light shines upon you and into the temple from the circular window before you, and you see that you are gazing into a landscape on an early morning in Spring, with the sun just rising above the horizon before you. Be aware of the singing of the dawn chorus of birds and of the diamond and rainbow scintillations of the dew upon the grass that begins to evaporate in the first beams of the morning sun, though some remain to outline with crystalline brilliance the occasional spider's web, the drops like the crystallization of the worlds at the dawn of creation.

See just before the window a low altar upon which is a small dagger in a richly embroidered sheath. Take this up and draw the dagger, retaining the sheath in your other hand. Hold the dagger pointing upward and outward before you as if pointing to far goals or horizons, and hold the sheath, whose sigils contain the wisdom on how to use the dagger of spiritual initiative, immediately before your heart.

As you stand there, a large triangle of golden light begins to appear in the window space before you, point upwards, and with a golden bar across its center, parallel to its base. This is the Triangle of Air. You then see a figure building in the air at each one of its points, outside the space of the triangle. At the topmost point is the figure of a handsome man or god holding a pitcher of water which he is pouring down all round the triangle, as if these were the waters of life with which he is fertilizing a garden. Now see at the bottom left corner two children appear, like twin brother and sister, dancing in a fairy ring in the grass before a low wall behind which flowers blossom, rather like the Tarot Trump of the Sun. Then in the lower right hand corner of the triangle see the figure of a young woman build, throned and blindfolded and holding a sword in one hand, and prominently before her in the other a pair of scales, its pans swinging in equilibrium from the knife edge balance point; again similar to the Trump of Justice in the Tarot.

These figures at the three corners of the triangle of air represent the zodiacal signs of Aquarius, Gemini and Libra, respectively. Now, within the space of the triangle itself, see the figures of a fairy king and a fairy queen appear in the air, and dancing in the breezes all about them the whirling figures of sylphs, the traditional elemental creatures of air. You may vibrate the traditional name of their ruler — Paralda — to see them immediately burst into a dance of even greater activity.

You may stand contemplating this scene for as long as you wish. Then, in your own time, sheath the dagger and place it back upon the low altar before you, when the triangle and its figures will begin to fade. Then with the imagined or physically stated formula, "In the name of Jod-Heh-Vau-Heh, Raphael and Paralda I close the gates of the East," step backward a pace and draw the curtains between the pillars closed.

Go back to the central altar, and this time with your back to the East and facing West, perform the Qabalistic Cross, giving due intention of respect and thanksgiving to Sandalphon and go towards the Guide who stands at the door to lead you from this temple back down the spiral stairs.

It is probably enough that you devote the evocation of just one elemental quarter of the temple to each visit, although you should maintain a balanced routine by visiting each quarter in turn. The following instructions apply to the southern, western and northern quarters on subsequent visits.

For the southern quarter, having performed the opening Qabalistic Cross at the central altar standing on the northern side of it and facing south, proceed toward the russet red curtains and in making the sign of the pentagram vibrate the angelic name Michael (pronounced Mee-kah-el). Open the curtains between the pillars with the Holy Name of Adonai (pronounced Ah-doh-nah-ee).

This time you will find that the warm and bright light of the noon day sun shines in upon you and that you are gazing upon a summer landscape with growth burgeoning throughout it in the trees and grasses and flowers with bees humming from hives gathering in the nectar of the blossoms along with the colored fluttering flight of butterflies.

Upon the low altar that stands before the window you will find a short magic wand of hazel wood carved into a form of intertwining strands about a central shaft and bearing a dark tetrahedral stone at each end. That is to say, a pyramidal figure of four triangular sides. Take up the wand and hold it immediately before you, and with your hand that holds its center before your throat, you will find that its lower end is before your heart and the upper end at your brow. At the same time the lower stone of the wand glows with a dark green emerald light and the upper end a brilliant purple amethyst.

Magical Images and the Magical Imagination

As before, a triangle begins to appear before you in the window, only this time without a bar across its center. This is the Triangle of Fire. A figure begins to form at each point. This time at the top is the head of a lion, fierce and roaring at first, which slowly transforms into the figure of a young maiden leading it docilely with a chain made out of flowers, rather after the fashion of the Tarot Trump known as Strength. At the bottom left hand corner of the triangle there appears a centaur who holds a bow and arrow which he points upwards to fire over a rainbow. And at the bottom right is the figure of a ram, with golden fleece, looking round behind it as if to lead its flock. These have their zodiacal equivalents in the astrological signs of Leo, Sagittarius and Aries.

Now, within the triangle, see the figures of a fiery masculine and feminine couple, the rulers of the salamanders, transforming creatures of fire, that writhe like lizards within the glow of a furnace and yet give an impression of power and wisdom, as if pictures of great wisdom and empowerment might be seen in their fire, which is as the heart of the sun. You may here vibrate the name of their ruler, Djinn, to see greater activity within their movement and possibly greater revelation within their fires.

When you are ready, return the wand to the altar, where its stones will cease to glow and the visions begin to fade. On closing the russet curtains do so with the formula "In the name of Adonai, Michael and Djinn I close the gates of the South." Then return to the center and close as before.

For evocation of the powers of the western quarter, you start at the eastern side of the central altar, facing West and perform the Qabalistic Cross before moving to the olive green curtains between the western pillars. The angelic name here is Gabriel, pronounced Gah-bree-el, and the traditional Divine Name AHIH, or Eheieh (pronounced Ay-hay-ay-ay).

*As you open the curtains, you will find the light ema-
nates from the sun setting in glory over the horizon of the
western sea, but as if seen from upstream of a river estuary
whereby you can see fields and orchards at the time of har-
vest home, at the season of mists and mellow fruitfulness.*

*Upon the low altar before the window will be a silver cup
containing wine, the fruit of the vine, and you may raise
this before you and visualize yourself drinking from the
cup in salutation to the setting sun and in thanks for the
fruits of the earth. Then, as you stand with the cup held
before you, see appearing through the window before you,
with the sea for its background, the Triangle of Water. This
is a plain equilateral triangle that has its point downward.
At the downward point you will see appear the form of a
lobster or crayfish, the marine form of the astrological sign
of Scorpio, the scorpion, that holds its claws out and upward before it in a way reminiscent of the balances of the
scales of justice, and its tail curled up slightly at the end.
To the upper right you will see a couple of fishes swim-
ming in a circle, one silver and one gold, whose movement
suggests a vortex of polarity similar to the oriental "taigetu"
sign. And to the upper left see the form of a crab, of the
hermit variety, that emerges from a spiral shell. These figures represent the water signs of Scorpio, Pisces and Can-
cer respectively. Within the triangle, stimulated into activity as you vibrate the name of their ruler, Nixsa, you can
see a crowned mermaid and merman surrounded by water nymphs, or undines, in various forms and surrounded
by various sea creatures of evocative shapes, such as sea
horses, star fish or sea anemones, some of them perhaps
bearing undersea pearls or other treasures.*

*Close this vision in a similar way to the others, by re-
turning the cup to the small altar, and closing the curtains, to the accompaniment of the spoken formula: "In
the name of Eheieh, Gabriel and Nixsa I close the gates of
the West."*

Magical Images and the Magical Imagination

The ceremonial form for opening the northern quarter follows the pattern that has gone before. Commence at the southern side of the central altar, facing North. When you go to the dark curtains of the North do so in the divine name of AGLA, an acrostic formula that means "Thou art mighty for ever, O Lord," and is pronounced Ah-Glah, whilst the relevant archangel is Uriel (pronounced Oo-ree-el).

Upon opening these curtains you will see through the circular window the night sky, brilliant with stars. You may see high before you the pole star, Polaris, with the constellations of the Dragon and the Great and Little Bears revolving round it. Not far away will be a band of light that is the Milky Way. You may be aware also of a darkened landscape before you which is invisible save for the presence of lights of homes and streets and towns that are reflections, in a sense, of the stars above.

Upon the small altar before you will be a golden disc upon which is engraved a series of concentric circles emblematic of the crystalline spheres of the heavens surrounding the Earth. As you pick up this talisman and hold it before you, its circles scintillate with rainbow light of the gems set within it and the very metal of the disc begins to glow in your hands.

And through the window you will see the formation of the Triangle of Earth, downward pointing with a horizontal bar across it. At the bottom point you will see arise the figure of a bull, immensely powerful. Its head alone appears at first but then you may see its whole body in profile, in the form of an ox pulling a mighty plough through the earth. At the upper right the figure of a maiden, who stands among sheaves of corn, and who holds aloft a single ear of corn. And at the upper left the figure of a goat, that appears to plunge out of the sea at the foot of a mountain, and to leap agilely from crag to crag, to stand upon its topmost peak gazing at the stars.

Temples and Shrines

Upon your invoking the name Ghob (pronounced Gobe), the ruler of the elemental beings of Earth, you will see the activation of a king and queen of the underworld regions of the earth, in an underground cavern sparkling with gems, and surrounded with gnomes and similar workers within the secret chambers of the earth itself, mining precious metals and stones, and guarding stores of treasure.

When you close down this vision by replacing the golden disc upon the altar use the spoken formula "In the name of Agla, Uriel and Ghob, I close the gates of the North."

*****

We have now gained some experience of the interior of a magical temple or lodge. We have of course sampled only a small proportion of all possible symbolism that might be met with, but what we have seen and worked with so far gives a general pattern upon which much more can be added as knowledge and experience develops. All this range of adventure and development is open to the career of the magical student as experience develops. What we have done is to map out the basic dynamics, in a self balancing four fold pattern, that will allow a great deal more symbolism to be built around it.

There are limits, however, to the use of this kind of mostly inanimate and abstract imagery, and the next stage of the use of the magical imagination it to use it in a more dynamic manner with symbolism that is intelligent, animate and more consciously interactive. This has to do with the formulation and contact of various guides.

We have already sampled something of this in form of the figures that we have met upon the way in our inner journeys, but this has been at a somewhat formal distance, in their form as archetypes of symbolic offices rather than

67

personal contacts in their own right. Our next step therefore is to endeavour to come onto more intimate terms with these focuses of intelligent consciousness upon the inner planes. These may appear in various forms: as totem animals or human guides, or elemental and angelic intelligences of various kinds.

Note: More detailed instruction on drawing the cross and the pentagram as well as other aspects of the symbolism of the magical temple will be found in my *Practice of Ritual Magic* (Sun Chalice, 1996).

Chapter 5

Guardians and Guides

We have so far learned how to tap the forces of our own aura and to guide our inner energies into forms that, by the process of magical journeys and the formulation of magical shrines, give us a basis for intelligent work upon the inner planes.

So far, however, our work has been mostly with inanimate objects, with the images of landscape and of buildings and of symbols within temple constructs. There is another important factor in all of this, and that is the presence of animate beings, intelligent sources of guidance and possibly more detailed communication.

It is possible, but unusual, to have an entirely inanimate magical inner scenario. In the work we have done so far we found it helpful to take account of birdsong along the trackway as part of our Composition of Mood and of Place. And when we arrived at the tower we met with various animate beings. There was the crowd within the Hall of Welcoming, and more specifically the Smith and the Hermit who took us to the lower levels of the tower, and then the Guide who took us up the spiral stairway and oversaw our efforts with the Temple of the Elements.

Each in their way, these figures fulfilled a specific role, as guardian of a particular place and guide to its working.

The simplest form of guide has traditionally been an animal form. This has its parallel in animal totems of various tribal peoples but it has its expression at many levels of being.

One technique that is favored is to visualize a small animal coming to us as we meditate upon an out of door scenario, perhaps a cave or forest edge. The species of the small animal is a matter of spontaneous choice or individual intuition. For some it may be a domestic creature, such as dog or cat, for others a wild one such as wolf or stag or bear or wise bird. There is no restriction on the type of animal that may appear save the limits of the imagination.

The animal may then lead the way onto an inner journey to a particular shrine or place. When we have been taken to that place the totem animal may then stand as guard outside, waiting to lead us back the way we came, after we have finished our work at the place to which we have been led.

Many examples exist in myth, legend and folklore. An important one that figures in Arthurian legend is that of a king or knight following a stag or a white hart. The animal leads the king or knight far into the forest, away from all his companions until it turns upon its now lone pursuer and exhibits some marvellous property. It may speak, or display some numinous symbol between the branches of its horns. A wild boar is also a common tutelary animal in this kind of story and can lead the hunter into a remote part of an enchanted forest, there to meet some faery being, perhaps a form of the goddess.

One famous example of such is the story of Yvain, or the Knight of the Lion, first recorded by the medieval French *romancier*, Chrétien de Troyes, and which appears also in an ancient Welsh tale included in the collection called *The Mabinogion* as "The Knight of the Fountain." Here the hero going through the forest is first met and entertained by a young maiden and her widowed father in a castle, where he spends the night, chastely, although not without some hint of romance. The next morning they direct him on his way in search of adventure and he comes upon a giant and grotesque being who is Lord of the Wild Creatures, a sort of guardian over all animal guides (as such he is sometimes likened to the magician Merlin). This being then directs Yvain to the site of the magic fountain.

Here there is an emerald stone set upon four rubies in a stream with a golden cup by its side. He is instructed to pour water from the stream over the stone. As soon as he does so a mighty storm erupts, which, when it has passed, gives way to a paradisal scene with the sun shining and the branches of the trees covered with singing birds. But then a fierce red knight comes galloping up to challenge the newcomer, who if he overcomes this guardian is destined to take his place and become the consort of the faery lady of the fountain.

This story goes back to very ancient rites and times when sacred places were actually physically guarded in this manner by an armed priest guardian. Sir James Frazer gives an example of one such in *The Golden Bough*. Traditions change according to need and circumstance however, and in Chrétien de Troyes' 12th century version of the story, things become more complicated, and another magical creature appears in the form of a lion which helps the knight in his adventures.

You will waste no time in reading widely of myth and legend along these lines for they will stimulate and enrich your magical imagination. This includes all forms of folk lore and fairy stories, whether intended for children or adults.

Talking animals play a major role in many children's stories, although there is little direct magical element in the nursery whimsy of some of the tales. However, Mowgli, the jungle boy of Rudyard Kipling comes close to the mark, and there are many instances, particularly in more traditional tales, where we are very definitely involved with a magical guide, whether it be fish, flesh or fowl.

There is an intermediate category between the animal guide and the human, in the form of one of the "little folk" as elf or pixie or gnome. A classic example is that of the overseer of the time travels of the children in Kipling's *Puck of Pook's Hill*. Whether Kipling realized it or not, his story starts with the elements of a magical working. The children are at a specific location associated with the past, a riverside by an old mill (which still stands, for those interested enough to visit his former home of "Batemans" in East Sussex, which is owned by the National Trust and is now open to the public).

The children are performing an evocation of sorts in that they are dressed up, enacting the fairy parts of *A Midsummer Night's Dream*, and this has the unexpected side effect of evoking to visible appearance the elemental guardian of the place. He teaches them something of their magical and cultural heritage by taking them back through time to previous events in the district, including contacts with the pagan gods such as Weland the Smith. The means by which this is done is by a short evocation of the three tree powers of oak and ash and thorn.

Kipling found a kindred spirit, and indeed inspiration for much of his involvement in this kind of magical literature, ostensibly for children, in Edith Nesbit, whose *The Children and It* (originally called *The Psammead*) gives an evocative series of tales with a non-human, non-animal creature, who is able to take them to levels of being off the normal physical plane of experience. Other books of hers involve the children in similar adventures with a phoenix, with an amulet, and with a princess in an enchanted castle. Edith Nesbit had a fairly clear idea of what she was doing from her membership in the Hermetic Order of the Golden Dawn.

Another Golden Dawn related teller of children's tales is P. L.Travers, the author of the Mary Poppins stories, whose original Mary Poppins was more in the nature of a pagan tutelary goddess than as depicted in the later film, as was quickly recognized by magical aficionados of her acquaintance such as the mystical Irish poets W.B.Yeats and George Russell ("A.E.").

A magical type of children's fiction has become an important genre in its own right in the decades since Kipling, Nesbit and Travers wrote, and has developed branches appealing directly to adults as for instance in the works of Tolkien.

However the "magical" appeal to the imagination does not stop there, for it can spill over into many kinds of fantasy literature, whether dealing with angelic beings, high elven creatures, ancient civilizations or beings from outer space. It might be said that the twentieth century has been a time when a sustained effort has been made to expand the mind of the general public with "mind stretching" forms of entertainment such as this. Started in English fiction in 1895 by H.G.Wells with *The War of the Worlds* and *The Time Machine* and so on, and later being adapted to screen and television performance, there is reason to believe that there is some sort of inner purpose in this influx of the marvellous into popular culture.

Not that writers of such material are, by any means, practicing magicians, but they are sufficiently imaginative to use their minds in as free and creative a way as any magical student should. Indeed it is arguable that there is as much esoteric truth to be found in contemporary genre fiction as in the learned wisdom teachings of esoteric societies. If this is the case, it is nothing new, for in former times presentations of popular games such as the Tarot contained powerful esoteric information. Magic, therefore, is where you find it, and there is a tradition of presenting esoteric truths in disguised form that goes back at least as far as Apuleius of Madaura's classic comic novel *The Golden Ass*, which at a deeper level is an exposition of the ancient Mysteries of Isis.

Truth can indeed be stranger than fiction, and may sometimes best be presented in the form of fiction. And as often as not, this is through the intuitive insights and subconscious or superconscious promptings that come to popular authors as they delve into their minds for stories. The moral for any esoteric student is to read widely and deeply in imaginative fiction. Much may be ephemeral or inconsequential, but that which is good is likely to stay within your mind as it strikes a resonance with your deeper faculties.

However, to return to the straighter and narrower way of the mainstream of esoteric teachings there is a pantheon of contacts that has come to the fore in much the same period of time as the growth of magical and fantasy fiction. These beings are generally referred to as the Masters, and although their existence was popularized in the late nineteenth century by the publications of the Theosophical Society they are by no means their exclusive invention. Rosicrucian and Masonic documents of the seventeenth century make clear reference to such beings, as do early Jewish Qabalistic writings, where such a contact was called a *maggid*.

In the modern presentation of this type of being a more specific description has been given of some of them, though perhaps their precise form should not be taken in quite so rigid and literal a sense as the stone that Dr. Johnson kicked to prove the existence of solid matter. Various schools and writers have since taken up the running and gone on to make their own contacts and publish the results, with varying degrees of worth and credibility.

Taking some of the general descriptions at face value, we might come up with a college of inner teachers of wisdom, who measure up something like this:

The Master Rakoczi, sometimes referred to as the Count, and identified or associated with the 18th century Count Cagliostro and the 17th century Francis Bacon. Also credited in other literature with being the Lord of Civilization, a kind of inner plane function that might be generally equivalent to a kind of inner plane Secretary General of the United Nations.

The English Master, whom some have identified with Sir Thomas More, Lord Chancellor of England under Henry VIII, who has contrived the distinction of also being a Roman Catholic saint and martyr. The poet Robert Browning is another Englishman reckoned by some to be of Master status. As also David Carstairs, an otherwise unknown officer in the British army of the First World War, whose very existence is denied by some biographers, but who has been responsible for some very lively communications.

The Greek philosopher Socrates also appears from time to time, not only in rather abstract philosophical dissertations but in rather more earthly types of contact in keeping with his personality as revealed in the works of Plato, and his jocular comparison to Silenas, an ancient satyr follower of Bacchus.

There is a selection of Himalayan-based Masters credited with being behind much of the Theosophical teachings of Madame Blavatsky, not least *The Secret Doctrine* and *Isis Unveiled*. Of these the Master Morya and the Master Jupiter (whom some link together) have a strong power contact, whilst Koot Hoomi is a more gentle influence. Somewhat junior in the Blavatsky pantheon was a Tibetan who has subsequently been credited with a great mass of teaching published by Alice A. Bailey, under the name of Djwal Khul.

The Master Serapis, has Alexandrian Greek connections and has also been used as a channel for elemental and what would nowadays be regarded as "green" concerns, whilst the Master Hilarion has been known to respond to workings of Egyptian magic, as well as in more general communications.

In the modern climate of the importance of feminine power and responsibility it may be asked why all the above mentioned communicators should be male. We suggest that this is not necessarily evidence of sexist chauvinism upon the inner planes, but owes much to the historical context from which we are quoting. Also to be taken into account is that those who made these contacts upon the physical plane were almost always women, so there may well be an element of cross-gender polarity involved in the psychological process of inner plane communication. Not necessarily essential, but possibly helpful.

Be this as it may, in our own approach to these matters we may expect to receive that which we aspire to by our own creative ideas and ideals. The process of communication is like a painted veil, and the pictures upon the veil are painted by us, by means of our own imagination. This does not mean to say that there are no real beings beyond the veil, willing to communicate by means of the pictures we have mutually created in the astral light.

The Masters as we picture them, along with the rest of magical imagery, are all imagination. But that does not mean to say that they are figments of fancy, wish fulfillment or otherwise. If we form an image, and believe in it sufficiently to invest it with some emotive force, then that same image can be overlaid with a similar imaginative projection by an inner plane contact. Once that happens then genuine conscious contact between the planes is possible.

It might be said that this process is automatically followed by many religious devotees, of whatever faith, in their approach to their God or gods or saints, without any conscious concern with magical technique. In this sense, magic is not an cultish minority interest, but a practice that embraces a very wide spectrum of human experience.

The specialist nature of the magical approach is that it attempts a more conscious and detailed form of communication between the planes than is the case with the more generalized approach of the religious devotee.

This does not mean to say that any detailed communication received is going to be fool proof, or even wholly accurate. In mind to mind contacts subjective dubbing in from the subconscious mind of the recipient is a constant factor. This is only to be expected in that the communicator is trying to use the contents of the subconscious mind of the recipient as a kind of word processor keyboard. When we are attempting such a process we are inviting someone else, the communicator, to think our thoughts for us, or at any rate to direct them. It follows that if we have limited ideas and experience, or our minds are distorted with prejudice or preconceptions, then any communication will be to that extent limited or distorted.

The large proportion of alleged communications that obviously fall short in this respect demonstrate that this is an almost universal problem. One communicator once likened the process to trying to making a picture with feathers, which the slightest draught could disturb, sometimes quite radically. Another has asserted that only 2% of alleged communications are likely to be valid.

However, even if charlatans, dabblers or early learners make up 98% of what has come to be called "channelled" material, that does not mean to say that 2% do not succeed in getting it right. Our problem lies in identifying that crucial minority. Or in more practical terms, sifting the wheat from the chaff in that grey area in between, where communications are like the curate's egg, good or bad in parts. Like long distance radio communication there can be all kinds of interference and fading of signals through inner atmospherics, and inner plane communication has much in common with ham radio.

Some recipients of such communication have worked in full trance, sometimes without any revelation as to who their alleged communicator might be, nor with very much conscious sympathy with the process as a whole. One such remarkable case was the claivoyant Edgar Cayce, who as a conservatively religious man when conscious, did not really have a lot of sympathy with the kind of things he received when he fell into trance, except insofar that they genuinely seemed to help others who came for advice or healing.

It is not our intention to try to teach trance mediumship by means of a book, even if that were possible. As far as higher communications are concerned it is a form of working that is largely superceded. However, the occultist Dion Fortune in a series of early articles in a magazine for her students, did feel it worthwhile to describe the way she went about it. This remains of interest, because the initial stages of the method are very similar to those which we should apply in attempting direct mind to mind telepathic inner contact, without relapsing into the unconscious passive state of mediumistic trance.

As far as she was concerned, the first essentials were complete physical relaxation, relative quietness and subdued light. She found the lowered level of lighting very important, and a condition which seemed to affect the whole aura, for simply blindfolding the eyes was no solution to a problem of too much light. Indeed, any sudden bright light was more disturbing and disruptive even than a sudden loud noise. Once she had got into a trance condition any more or less steady background noise was largely immaterial.

She would then build up in her imagination a picture of the being she wished to contact. This was not just a matter of hard mental concentration, but passing beyond that to what might best be described as a state of almost hypnotic fascination, as in bystanders who have witnessed an accident. All consciousness of the surrounding room would then blank out as she would find herself in full trance.

This could be accompanied by some rather odd sensations. A sense of squinting in the eyes, perhaps due to the eyeballs turning upward as in deep sleep. Then a feeling of going down quickly in a lift. She would blank out for a moment before being aware of herself floating a couple of feet above her physical body, wrapped up like a mummy. Although occasionally, in particularly deep trance, she would find herself standing upright behind the head of her prone physical body, facing the communicator, who was standing by her physical body's feet.

Communication would then commence, and this would tend at first to push consciousness back into her physical body. This was overcome by the will of her own higher consciousness and that of the communicator preventing her lower consciousness from doing so — a process she rather amusingly described as being somewhat like trying to get a reluctant horse into a railway van!

What followed then depended upon the action of the communicator, which was to build up an image of himself and superimpose it upon the medium's body upon the couch, whose vocal chords he would proceed to use to speak to those physically assembled.

Dion Fortune likened this technique to a form of self hypnosis with the inner communicator taking the part of an unseen hypnotist. When the work in hand was finished she would wake as from a deep sleep remembering very little, and sometimes nothing, of what had occurred. After a certain amount of minor physical discomfort she would find herself considerably invigorated by the experience.

It should be said it took Dion Fortune considerable practice over a number of years to perform all this with ready facility. Apart from this we must remember it also takes two to tango. That is to say, the presence of a communicator willing to come through in this way. It has gone on record that such close association with an entranced physical body is not a wholly pleasant experience, and a matter of duty rather than a pleasure, although most would be too polite to say so. The celebrated remark of one, that the medium's body smelled like an old cough drop, was somewhat by way of an exception.

There has, over the years, been a general rise in consciousness and acceptance of the reality of inner plane communications, so that some of these heroic efforts by pioneering souls are no longer necessary. A more conscious telepathic or mind-to-mind contact is favored today, with the recipient fully conscious and seated, rather than prone and unconscious.

Nonetheless, a similar modus operandi is involved in the earlier stages, except that the degree of fascinated concentration that brought about projection of consciousness out of the physical body is no longer required. The communicator takes no direct control of physical or etheric organs of the medium, and in token of this the term *medium* has rather given place to *mediator*. The process therefore becomes entirely a matter of conscious visualization, not dissimilar from the state of mind of a creative writer.

Once a rapport has been built up in conscious cooperation between master and mediator, then there is little mistake about what is happening or any doubts about the reality of the situation. Dion Fortune described the approach of a master as a curious sense of power beginning to develop as if one were waiting for a race to start. With this could come an intuitive awareness as to whom the communicator was likely to be, she being accustomed to work on a regular basis with more than one.

The validity of any communication depends very much on what might be described as the coalescing of the aura of the master with that of the mediator. This is partly a matter of practice, and partly a matter of natural ability, as in any human skill or creative art. The key to success lies in the principle of *like mindedness*.

It is an esoteric axiom, well proven by experience, that upon the inner planes "Like attracts Like." If therefore we are in sympathy with the aims and expressions of a particular teacher, then we are by that measure more closely attuned to his aura. The practical corollary to this is that if we desire to make an inner contact of any particular kind then we should steep ourselves in whatever appropriate writings we can find that stem from that or a similar source. This is another form of the technique of tuning consciousness.

Magical Images and the Magical Imagination

Esoteric groups perpetuate themselves in this way. Members of the up and coming generation, being instilled with the teaching from the contacts of those who have gone before, are the better placed to make such contacts for themselves. Thus the light of illumination is passed on in that particular school or working group. If, for whatever reason, a hiatus should develop between one generation and another, as long as written material is available, a dedicated individual can use it to renew the contact, and blow the seeming dead ashes into flame.

This can also be helped by knowing the identity of the alleged communicator, so that the visual imagination can be brought to bear in picking up a contact.

In mind to mind communication a problem often arises with the speed with which material comes through, generally twice or three times the rate that would normally be expected if the mediator were working off his or her own resources. Sometimes it may come through more slowly and deliberately in a word for word dictation, but at other times it will come through in small blocks of ideas that have to be instantly rendered into the most appropriate language. At such times the process is very much like taking fast dictation in one language and translating it immediately into another.

Grammar and spelling obviously tend to go by the board in such cases, and also felicity of phrasing and sentence length. This at least needs to be put into order by such light editing as may be necessary. Wherever such communications are destined for wider publication though, particularly in book form, then rather more editing is needed. On the one hand to make the reading easier for those who may not be so committed to teasing out the meaning of complex phraseology; on the other hand to forestall those critics who would readily confuse lack of good English with ignorance or incompetence. However it has to be said that the more editing involved, even by the person who received the material in the first place, the less of the original "power" of communication comes across.

This matter of power of communication is allied to what Dion Fortune described as the subtle change in the atmosphere that occurs when genuine inner contact is about to take place. It can also happen that the intention behind a particular communication is not primarily in the intellectual content of the message. The intention may be more one of comfort, encouragement or some form of subtle empowerment. In such cases the intellectual content of the communication may be little more than general spiritual commonplace remarks, not necessarily destined for wider publication.

To recapitulate, let us try to draw together some guides for personal action from all these elements that we have considered.

We have established that we can meet beneficent inner guides through the medium of our active imagination. And the power and suitability of these guides can be selected, or filtered out, by means of using a traditional symbolic inner environment for them, that we also build in the mind's eye.

If we wish to do so, we may then spend some time in concentrating upon the presence of such a guide, building him — or her — in the creative imagination, getting the general "feel" of the presence of the inner guide, and waiting to see if any message is expressed.

Messages can come to you in many ways. They may be in the form of words that formulate spontaneously in your mind, or perhaps just a bright idea that springs to life as you contemplate the image of the guide. As an aid to prime the pump, so to speak, it is a very good idea to hold a question in your mind to see if you get an answer. This sets up the most basic form of polarity. And indeed the same principles apply as in outer life, if you wish to start or maintain a conversation then the best way is to ask a question.

It may be thought that all this seems somewhat risky stuff, rather like training yourself into the symptoms of split personality. However the difference between creative visualization and schizophrenia is one of control. The schizophrenic is a victim of hallucinations. We are talking of the controlled use, under will, of our creative powers.

The development of the magical imagination is no different, in essence, from the process cultivated by every imaginative writer and creative artist. Indeed the techniques that we have described could well be used as training for freeing the mind in any form of creative writing.

There is no doubt that some writers are "guided" or inspired, whether they realize it or not. And it is quite a common occurrence for writers to feel that their characters "take over" the story. This is not necessarily the same as occult mediation, in which the crucial factor is whether there is a spiritual teacher of merit behind the imaginations involved. But the psychological mechanism is very similar. What matters is who is in the driving seat. And this can be a variety of possibilities from an element in the writer's subconscious to a tuning into some element in the collective unconscious, which might well produce a work of genius irrespective of any esoteric or spiritual content.

Seeking a Guide

The seeking of an inner spiritual guide is very much a personal matter, so our directions toward such a step must needs be fairly generalized. We will describe a general outline path or pattern to follow but it is up to you to fill in the detail according to your aspiration and own intuition.

Guardians and Guides

Starting at whatever point you wish in the journey to the tower which we have been using, see yourself being taken by the guide who conducted you to the temple of the elements to a higher storey in the tower. The top of the spiral staircase ends in a door, which he invites you to enter.

When you go through you find yourself in a circular room that is entirely surrounded by windows. The light is clear and comes from all sides, and through the windows you see nothing but the azure of the sky, with perhaps a few wispy clouds. You are above the level of sight of the earth and of the concerns of the tower below you.

The room is bare of furniture but for a small circular table in the center of white stone, with two chairs, one on either side that face each other. Sit yourself in one of the chairs. If you look up above you, you will see a circular skylight, in which can be seen not the blue of the sky around you, but what appears to be the sun, not exuding heat upon you, but shining with a clear diamond light. In a way, that white surface of the table before you is a reflection of the source of light.

You may now find that a book appears before you on the table, in which case you may open it, and regard any pictures that you may see within, or try to read any writing that may appear. Do not strain after this. If it happens, let it happen in its own way and own time, and record and reflect upon what you have seen.

It may be simply that words or ideas or pictures come into your head. If these seem to crystallize of their own accord, and are not psychological baggage of worries or preoccupations that you have brought into this room with you, then these too are worthy of reflection, for they may be another form of communication.

Do not be too much concerned with whom at this stage. The composition of place that you have made will ensure that your contact, even if not consciously recognized, is a valid one. And it can be that it emanates from the light above, which in one sense might be regarded as your personal Holy Guardian Angel.

At some stage you may find that the seat before you becomes occupied. And you can assist it in this way if you wish, by actively building a generalized figure, which you can take from any of the images in the treasurehouse of symbolism known as the Tarot. Be it the Magician, the Fool, the Hermit, the Emperor, the High Priestess, the Empress, or any of the others. They are capable of being utilized by any inner contact who wishes to set up a rapport with you.

Remember that it is you who are in control all the time, no matter how seemingly powerful or eminent a contact may appear to be. You can, at your leisure, simply rise from the table, look up to the bright light of the spirit above, knock upon the table, and leave the room. The guide at the door will see you safely on your way back to normal consciousness.

*****

We have now completed our survey of magical images and the magical imagination. You will see that what we have done is to make a journey into your own aura, into the etheric vehicle. Each of the stages on the way in the tower has been a specific part of that aura; not using it directly as in eastern yoga techniques but by making an objective correlative of it, and walking into that space and making contact with any beings we may find or build there.

There is an approximate correlative with both the Tree of Life and the chakras of the eastern system, but the correspondences are not exact, for we deal with spheres of influence rather than a rigid set of Chinese boxes.

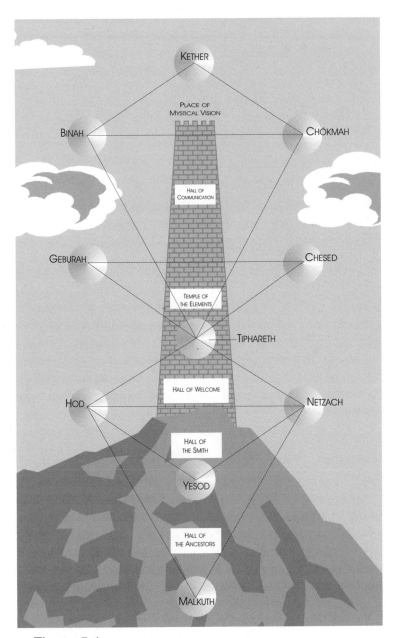

Figure 5.1

The Tower and the Tree of Life

Magical Images and the Magical Imagination

In general terms we enter into the Hall of Welcome more or less as a correlative of the solar plexus center, with the two lower centers as the Hall of the Smith and of the Ancestors, respectively. Then the Temple of the Elements relates to the heart and the Room of Communication to the throat, which will open up, as experience develops, into the head centers.

In terms of the Tree of Life it is probably better to think in terms of triangles of paths rather than specific Sephiroth. Thus the Hall of Welcome is the lower side of Tiphareth and the Temple of the Elements the higher, which can be thought of as the triangles between Hod-Netzach-Tiphareth and Chesed-Geburah-Tiphareth, if you will. The Smith's Hall is the triangle Netzach-Hod-Yesod and the Place of the Ancestors the inner side of Netzach-Hod-Malkuth. The Hall of Communication can be seen as commencing like the triangle between Chokmah, Binah and Tiphareth which is capable of transformation to that between Chokmah, Binah and Kether in the light of experience of the higher modes of inner communication. In Figure 5.1 we give an outline view of the ground we have covered.

We have now shown you the way through the plethora of magical symbolism in as concise a manner as we think possible. It is now up to you to use your magical imagination in practical steps to tread that way. Thus may imagination transform into reality, and aspiration be elevated into service. God's will be done.

Index

Index

OTHER GREAT TITLES FROM SUN CHALICE!

PATTERNS IN MAGICAL CHRISTIANITY
by Nicholas Whitehead

Magical Christianity is a means of bringing about spiritual transformation. This refers to both a mystical transfiguration of the soul, and to an active participation in the mediation of Divine Love, Power and Wisdom to little suspected inner aspects of creation. Contact with such inner realities is achieved through the imaginative use of symbolic material—images, legends, myths, rites and ceremonies.

$12.95   192 pp.   ISBN 0-9650839-7-7

THE PRACTICE OF RITUAL MAGIC:
powerful aids to concentration and visualization
by Gareth Knight

A sensible and intelligent look at this ancient art as a means of self-transformation. Complete instructions for building up a magical ritual system, with practical advice on robes, symbols and temple furniture. Includes concise explanations of Telesmatic Images, Names of Power, the Law of Correspondences, and the Qabalistic Cross. A new revised edition of this classic introduction to the magical arts by a leading authority on the Western Inner Traditions.

$9.95   96 pp.   ISBN 0-9650839-8-5

THE LORD OF THE DANCE:
an essay in mysticism
by Anthony Duncan

This is a book with a difference. Like Robert Graves' *White Goddess* it almost wrote itself. And it is at the same time both traditional and revolutionary. It is traditional in that it is based firmly on the Christian Eucharist and the Holy Trinity, but revolutionary in some of its insights into the 'inner side' of creation. These range from spiritual 'power centers' to the communion of saints, and the concourse of holy angels.
'A beautiful and remarkable book, it calls man to a life of active and daring communion with the resurrected and living Lord of the Dance, the risen Christ.'—THE BEACON

$10.95   117 pp.   ISBN 0-9650839-5-0

OCCULT EXERCISES AND PRACTICES:
gateways to the four 'worlds' of occultism
by Gareth Knight
Systems of spiritual development abound, and it is often
difficult for the student to find a way through their complexi-
ties in the quest for spiritual fulfillment. This non-technical
guide to the general principles of spiritual development teaches
the techniques of occultism in the form of physical, astral,
mental, and spiritual exercises, with an appendix on psychic
self-defense. The exercises guide the novice towards the final
goal of all seekers — the achievement of a relationship with the
denizens of the inner planes, and ultimately, with the Living
God. Completely revised edition.
$9.95   92pp.   ISBN 0-9650839-6-9

THE SWORD IN THE SUN:
dialogue with an angel
by Anthony Duncan
Here is the record of a remarkable conversation between an
angel and a rather surprised Christian priest. It is notable for
its intelligent treatment of little understood esoteric subjects
and its insight into the evolution of consciousness and the
relationship between human consciousness and Divine Being.
The book covers subjects ranging from the rhythms and
patterns of nature to channeling, reincarnation, and the
relation of the Qabalah to the chakras.
$14.95   212 pp.   ISBN 0-9650839-4-2

Sun Chalice Books
3445 Caseras Drive
Oceanside
CA 92056
U.S.A.